SENTENCE BUILDING

WORKBOOK

THIS BOOK BELONGS TO

HOMIE DADDI
PUBLISHING BY PCRB

SCAN TO VISIT THE AUTHOR PAGE
or

CHECK OUT OUR FACEBOOK PAGE
facebook.com/HomieDaddi

COMPLETE THE SENTENCES BELOW BY WRITING THE MISSING WORD.
USE THE IMAGES AS CLUES FOR THE MISSING WORD.

MY MORNING ROUTINE

1. Every morning, I brush my _____.

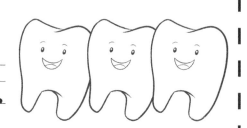

2. I take a bath and wash with _____.

3. I comb my _____.

4. I put on my _____.

3

ANSWER THE QUESTION BELOW BY
COMPLETING THE SENTENCE.

What does Alex like to wear?

Alex likes to wear a _____.

COMPLETE THE SENTENCES BELOW BY WRITING THE MISSING WORD.
USE THE IMAGES AS CLUES FOR THE MISSING WORD.

MY BREAKFAST

1. I eat breakfast at the _____.

2. I put cereal and _____ in my bowl.

3. The _____ is my favorite fruit.

4. I drink a _____ of water.

5

**ANSWER THE QUESTION BELOW BY
COMPLETING THE SENTENCE.**

What does Lulu like to play?

Lulu likes to play _____.

COMPLETE THE SENTENCES BELOW BY WRITING THE MISSING WORD.
USE THE IMAGES AS CLUES FOR THE MISSING WORD.

PLAY TIME

1. I play outside with my _____ .

2. We played with a _____ .

3. We played with a _____ .

4. We _____ down on the grass.

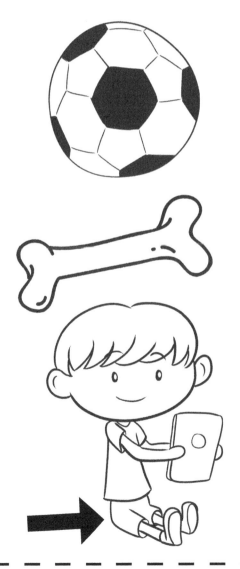

7

ANSWER THE QUESTION BELOW BY
COMPLETING THE SENTENCE.

What did Siel bake?

Siel baked a _____.

COMPLETE THE SENTENCES BELOW BY WRITING THE MISSING WORD.
USE THE IMAGES AS CLUES FOR THE MISSING WORD.

READING STORIES

1. I like _____ stories with my mother .

2. I have a favorite _____ _____ .

3. It tells a story about a _____ .

4. We read it before we go to _____ .

ANSWER THE QUESTION BELOW BY
COMPLETING THE SENTENCE.

What does Seven like to eat?

Seven likes to eat _____.

COMPLETE THE SENTENCES BELOW BY WRITING THE MISSING WORD.
USE THE IMAGES AS CLUES FOR THE MISSING WORD.

EATING FRUITS

1. My favourite fruit is the _____.

2. I like to eat cereal with_____ .

3. In the summer, we eat _____.

4. I like sweet red _____.

ANSWER THE QUESTION BELOW BY COMPLETING THE SENTENCE.

What is Matt doing?

Matt is typing on a _____.

COMPLETE THE SENTENCES BELOW BY WRITING THE MISSING WORD.
USE THE IMAGES AS CLUES FOR THE MISSING WORD.

EATING VEGETABLES

1. I like to eat fresh
_____
_____ .

2. I put a sliced _____
in my sandwich.

3. My mother makes
_____
_____ soup.

4. I like crunchy
_____
_____ .

ANSWER THE QUESTION BELOW BY
COMPLETING THE SENTENCE.

What kind of pet does Reno have?

Reno has a pet _____.

COMPLETE THE SENTENCES BELOW BY WRITING THE MISSING WORD.
USE THE IMAGES AS CLUES FOR THE MISSING WORD.

SHEEP IN THE FARM

1. The _____ is my favorite animal.

2. The sheep has _____ legs.

3. The sheep lives in a _____.

4. The sheep lives with a _____.

ANSWER THE QUESTION BELOW BY
COMPLETING THE SENTENCE.

Where is Joe putting his things?
Joe is putting his things inside
his _____.

COMPLETE THE SENTENCES BELOW BY WRITING THE MISSING WORD.
USE THE IMAGES AS CLUES FOR THE MISSING WORD.

TIGER IN THE JUNGLE

1. The _____ is a big animal.

2. Tigers have sharp _____.

3. Their fur is colored _____ and orange.

4. The tiger has a long _____.

17

ANSWER THE QUESTION BELOW BY
COMPLETING THE SENTENCE.

What is Ben eating?

Ben is eating a _____.

COMPLETE THE SENTENCES BELOW BY WRITING THE MISSING WORD.
USE THE IMAGES AS CLUES FOR THE MISSING WORD.

THE WEATHER TODAY

1. There are white
_____ in the sky.

2. The _____ is bright.

3. It does not look like
it will _____ today.

4. We saw a colorful
_____ .

ANSWER THE QUESTION BELOW BY
COMPLETING THE SENTENCE.

What does Mae have in her hand?

Mae has an _____.

COMPLETE THE SENTENCES BELOW BY WRITING THE MISSING WORD.
USE THE IMAGES AS CLUES FOR THE MISSING WORD.

BIRDS ON A TREE

1. The bird flew over the _____.

2. There is a _____ on the tree branch.

3. The bird uses its wings to _____.

4. This bird has long _____.

ANSWER THE QUESTION BELOW BY
COMPLETING THE SENTENCE.

How many cookies are on the plate?

There are _____ cookies.

COMPLETE THE SENTENCES BELOW BY WRITING THE MISSING WORD.
USE THE IMAGES AS CLUES FOR THE MISSING WORD.

IT'S A SNOW DAY

1. The weather today is
_____
_____ .

2. I have to wear a _____
on top of my head.

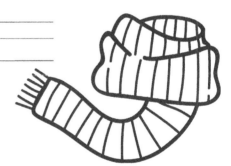

3. I am wearing a _____
around my neck.

4. I cover my hands
with _____ .

23

ANSWER THE QUESTION BELOW BY
COMPLETING THE SENTENCE.

What is Ken wearing on his head?

Ken is wearing a _____.

COMPLETE THE SENTENCES BELOW BY WRITING THE MISSING WORD.
USE THE IMAGES AS CLUES FOR THE MISSING WORD.

IT'S A RAINY DAY

1. It is _____ outside.

2. I will use an _____ if I go outside.

3. I will put on my _____.

4. I will wear my _____.

ANSWER THE QUESTION BELOW BY
COMPLETING THE SENTENCE.

What is Jim playing with?

Jim is playing with a _____.

COMPLETE THE SENTENCES BELOW BY WRITING THE MISSING WORD.
USE THE IMAGES AS CLUES FOR THE MISSING WORD.

A DAY AT THE BEACH

1. There is a red _____ on the beach.

2. It has _____ eyes.

3. It went out to the _____.

4. The crab is under an _____.

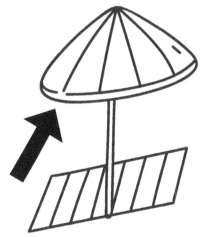

ANSWER THE QUESTION BELOW BY
COMPLETING THE SENTENCE.

What is Mia wearing on her head?

Mia is wearing a _____.

COMPLETE THE SENTENCES BELOW BY WRITING THE MISSING WORD.
USE THE IMAGES AS CLUES FOR THE MISSING WORD.

OUT IN THE GARDEN

1. I see a _____ in the garden.

2. The _____ smells good.

3. There is a _____ near the flowers.

4. I will _____ the plants.

ANSWER THE QUESTION BELOW BY
COMPLETING THE SENTENCE.

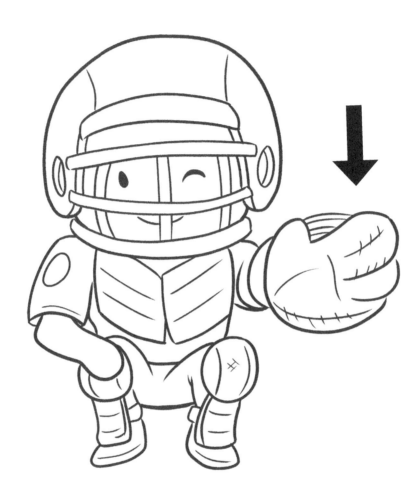

What is Jen wearing on her hand?

Jen is wearing a baseball _____.

COMPLETE THE SENTENCES BELOW BY WRITING THE MISSING WORD.
USE THE IMAGES AS CLUES FOR THE MISSING WORD.

THINGS THAT GO

1. We drove to the park in our _____.

2. We flew in an _____.

3. I know how to ride a _____.

4. We traveled by _____.

31

ANSWER THE QUESTION BELOW BY
COMPLETING THE SENTENCE.

Where does Liam like to play?

Liam likes to play on the _____.

COMPLETE THE SENTENCES BELOW BY WRITING THE MISSING WORD.
USE THE IMAGES AS CLUES FOR THE MISSING WORD.

CAT AND MOUSE

1. My friend has a
pet _____.

2. The cat chased a
_____
_____.

3. The cat likes to
eat _____.

4. The rat has
a long _____.

33

ANSWER THE QUESTION BELOW BY
COMPLETING THE SENTENCE.

How many fruits are on the tree?

There are _____ fruits

on the tree.

COMPLETE THE SENTENCES BELOW BY WRITING THE MISSING WORD.
USE THE IMAGES AS CLUES FOR THE MISSING WORD.

HAVING ICE CREAM

1. I want to eat some
_____
_____ .

2. I like _____
ice cream.

3. My friend likes
_____
_____ ice cream.

4. Ice cream feels cold
on my _____ .

ANSWER THE QUESTION BELOW BY
COMPLETING THE SENTENCE.

What is Rose holding?

Rose is holding a _____.

COMPLETE THE SENTENCES BELOW BY WRITING THE MISSING WORD.
USE THE IMAGES AS CLUES FOR THE MISSING WORD.

VISITING A FRIEND'S HOUSE

1. I visited my friend's _____.

2. I knocked on the _____.

3. They asked me to sit on the _____.

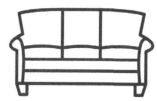

4. I took off my _____.

ANSWER THE QUESTION BELOW BY
COMPLETING THE SENTENCE.

How many kids are playing soccer?

There are _____ kids

playing soccer.

COMPLETE THE SENTENCES BELOW BY WRITING THE MISSING WORD.
USE THE IMAGES AS CLUES FOR THE MISSING WORD.

PLAYING OUTSIDE WITH A FRIEND

1. We were at my friend's _____.

2. We saw a _____ on a plant.

3. The bug was eating a _____.

4. There was an _____ on the ground.

ANSWER THE QUESTION BELOW BY
COMPLETING THE SENTENCE.

How many teacups are there?

There are _____ teacups.

COMPLETE THE SENTENCES BELOW BY WRITING THE MISSING WORD.
USE THE IMAGES AS CLUES FOR THE MISSING WORD.

MEETING A FRIEND'S PET

1. My friend has a pet
_____
_____ .

2. The rabbit likes to
eat _____ .

3. The rabbit likes
to _____ .

4. The rabbit has two
long _____ .

41

ANSWER THE QUESTION BELOW BY
COMPLETING THE SENTENCE.

What is Sara doing?

Sara is _____ tea.

COMPLETE THE SENTENCES BELOW BY WRITING THE MISSING WORD.
USE THE IMAGES AS CLUES FOR THE MISSING WORD.

THE FROG IN A POND

1. We went to see a _____ .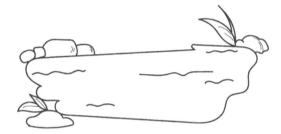

2. A green _____ lives inside the pond.

3. The frog is on a _____ .

4. It has a very long _____ .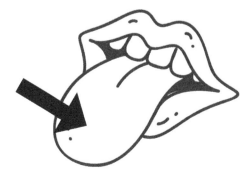

ANSWER THE QUESTION BELOW BY
COMPLETING THE SENTENCE.

What is Cris doing?

Cris is _____ a slice of pizza.

COMPLETE THE SENTENCES BELOW BY WRITING THE MISSING WORD.
USE THE IMAGES AS CLUES FOR THE MISSING WORD.

THE JUNGLE MONKEY

1. We read a _____ about animals.

2. A _____ can live in the jungle.

3. It can climb up the _____.

4. The monkey has a _____.

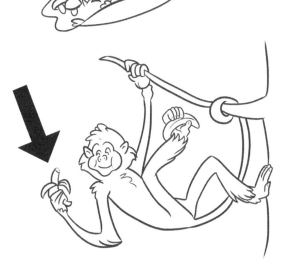

45

ANSWER THE QUESTION BELOW BY
COMPLETING THE SENTENCE.

How many kids are baking
in the kitchen?

There are _____ kids
baking in the kitchen.

COMPLETE THE SENTENCES BELOW BY WRITING THE MISSING WORD.
USE THE IMAGES AS CLUES FOR THE MISSING WORD.

THE CHICKEN IN THE FARM

1. There is a _____ in the farm.

2. The chicken lays _____.

3. A _____ hatched from the egg.

4. The chicken has _____ egg.

ANSWER THE QUESTION BELOW BY
COMPLETING THE SENTENCE.

How many kids are dancing?

There are _____ kids

dancing.

COMPLETE THE SENTENCES BELOW BY WRITING THE MISSING WORD.
USE THE IMAGES AS CLUES FOR THE MISSING WORD.

PLAYING WITH A BALL

1. The _____ is playing.

2. She is holding a _____ .

3. She hit the ball with a _____ .

4. The ball hit a _____ .

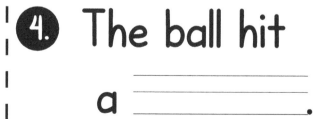

49

ANSWER THE QUESTION BELOW BY
COMPLETING THE SENTENCE.

How many kids are dancing?

There are _____ kids

dancing.

COMPLETE THE SENTENCES BELOW BY WRITING THE MISSING WORD.
USE THE IMAGES AS CLUES FOR THE MISSING WORD.

EATING CAKE

1. I want to eat some _____.

2. I will blow out the _____ on the cake.

3. The cake has _____ candles.

4. I will eat the cake with a _____.

ANSWER THE QUESTION BELOW BY
COMPLETING THE SENTENCE.

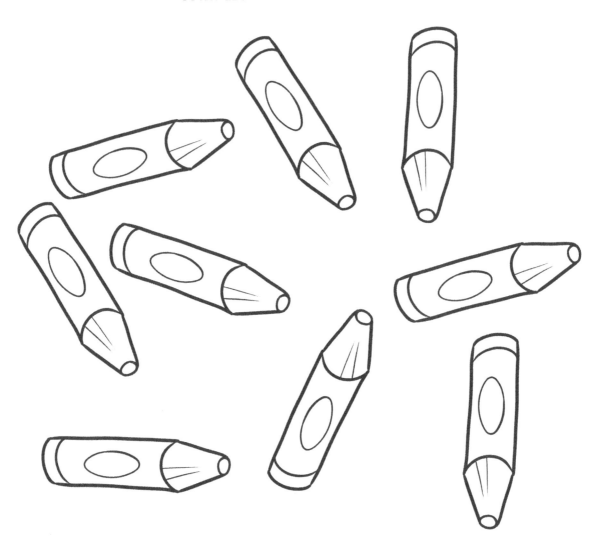

How many crayons are there?

There are _____ crayons.

COMPLETE THE SENTENCES BELOW BY WRITING THE MISSING WORD.
USE THE IMAGES AS CLUES FOR THE MISSING WORD.

GOING TO SCHOOL

1. I will bring my books to _____.

2. We ride the _____ to school.

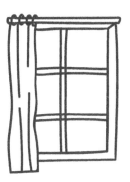

3. I sit beside the _____.

4. I sit on my _____ in the classroom.

ANSWER THE QUESTION BELOW BY
COMPLETING THE SENTENCE.

What kind of pet does Alice have?

Alice has a pet _____ .

COMPLETE THE SENTENCES BELOW BY WRITING THE MISSING WORD.
USE THE IMAGES AS CLUES FOR THE MISSING WORD.

GOING HOME

1. After class is over, it is _____ to go home.

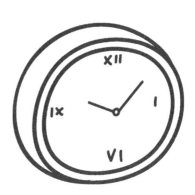

2. I pack my _____ and get ready to go home.

3. I wait for the _____ to pick me up.

4. I ride my family's _____ to go home.

ANSWER THE QUESTION BELOW BY
COMPLETING THE SENTENCE.

Where is Jason drawing?

Jason is drawing on a
piece of _____ .

COMPLETE THE SENTENCES BELOW BY WRITING THE MISSING WORD.
USE THE IMAGES AS CLUES FOR THE MISSING WORD.

NIGHT TIME

1. Look outside the _____.

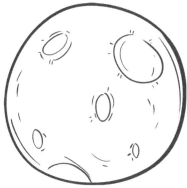

2. I can see the _____ outside.

3. There are _____ in the sky.

4. I will turn on the _____.

57

ANSWER THE QUESTION BELOW BY
COMPLETING THE SENTENCE.

What is Jazmin pulling?

Jazmin is pulling a cart

of _____ .

COMPLETE THE SENTENCES BELOW BY WRITING THE MISSING WORD.
USE THE IMAGES AS CLUES FOR THE MISSING WORD.

MY NIGHT TIME ROUTINE

1. I am getting ready for _____.

2. I _____ my teeth.

3. I lie my head on a _____ _____.

4. It is time to _____.

ANSWER THE QUESTION BELOW BY
COMPLETING THE SENTENCE.

What is Leo wearing?

Leo is wearing a pair
of _____ .

Made in the USA
Middletown, DE
21 September 2023

38890245R00038